19 MASKS for the NAKED POET

Poems by
NANCY WILLARD

Illustrated by
REGINA SHEKERJIAN

Harcourt Brace Jovanovich, Publishers

San Diego   New York   London

Library of Congress Cataloging in Publication Data

Willard, Nancy.
19 masks for the naked poet.

I. Title.   II. Title: Nineteen masks for the naked poet.
PS3573.I444A613 1984   811'.54   83-22734
ISBN 0-15-166039-5

Designed by Vaughn Andrews
Printed in the United States of America

First edition

A B C D E

For Jerry Badanes
and Jeriann Hilderly
—N.W.

For Tor and Jean-René
—R.S.

THE POET TAKES A PHOTOGRAPH OF HIS HEART

The doctor told him,
Something is living in your heart.
The poet borrowed a camera.
He told his heart to smile.
He slipped the plate under his ribs
and caught his heart running out of the picture.
He told his heart to relax.
It beat on the plate with its fist.
It did not want to lose its face!
He told his heart he was taking nothing
but an ikon by which to remember it.
Then the heart stood up like a bandstand
and the wren who lived under the eaves
left her nest and started
the long journey south.

THE POET RUNS A RACE
WITH THE BROOKLYN BRIDGE

The poet threw down his glove
on the Brooklyn Bridge.
"Bridge, run with me. I am the poet.
Faster than rivers, harder than steel,
though my legs are small and my belly a loaf."
The bridge cracked its sinews,
gathered its lean haunches
and together they flew over the needles
of industry, the steeples of Wall Street.
Children hid in their own shadows,
politicians praised Columbus,
the commuters gazed up at the face of God.
The Bridge got there first
but the poet won.

THE POET MEETS GOD
WHO IS RIDING ON A PIG

Because he has no money, the poet steals
a package of bacon from the A & P.
Then he meets, coming the other way
a man in a habit of light.
"Don't disturb this God you desire to eat,"
says the bacon in his hand.
"Hunger is stronger than letters,"
says the jade ring on his finger.
"Don't you recognize your father?"
say the shoes on his feet.
"You are walking too fast.
Prepare to meet your God,
to stable his pig,
to show him the stairs,
to dance with your wife,
to cry for your mother,
till your father's dust
finds its flesh again."

THE POET INVITES THE MOON FOR SUPPER

Tonight a stranger followed me home.
He wore an overcoat and feathers.
His head was as light as summer.
When I saw how much light he spilled
on the street, I knew he was rich.

He wanted to make me his heir.
I said, no thank you, I have a father.
He wanted to give me the snow to wife.
I said, no thank you, I have a sweetheart.
He wanted to make me immortal.
And I said, no thank you, but when you see
somebody putting me into the mouth
of the earth, don't fret.
I am a song.
Someone is writing me down.
I am disappearing into the ear of a rose.

THE POET PLANTS A FOREST
IN HIS WIFE'S MARIMBA

His wife had a sister, and the sister
sent a marimba.
It arrived with its hair in curling papers
and its back arched.
They petted it calm, it stretched like a dock
lying on deep water and bore
their blows for the tunes on its back.
A rosewood marimba!
A forest of roses!
He plays and remembers their names,
ROSA, ROSALINE, ROSEANNA, ROSEMARY,
and out of the wood they come,
rose trees with flowers like eyes,
with feet like pearls.
If you go in the evening to visit the poet,
you will see the roses
bringing him coffee, laying the table,
and singing his wife to sleep.

THE POET CALLS TO THE RADIO

Radio, sing me something.
And the radio says, What shall I sing?
And the poet replies, No matter,
sing me something.
Well, it sings from its guts.
Its tubes and filaments weep,
it tells its love, confesses its sins,
conjures the dark away with statistics and signs.
Like a goat it digests America.
Like an oven it warms to its subjects,
allows for all points of view,
and raises war to a high fragrance.
Well pleased, the poet pours it
his heart in a saucer.
And the radio naps at his feet.

BILLS FOR HORSES HE NEVER BOUGHT
AN INVENTORY OF STARS
A PLEA FOR HIS LEFT LEG
HE ANSWERS THEM ALL
SO BEAUTIFULLY THAT THE STABLEMAN
SAVES THE LETTER AND HANGS IT OVER HIS BED
THE AIR SAVES THE INVOICE AND SAYS IT ALOUD
THE ONE-LEGGED BEGGAR SAVES HIS REJECTION
AND EATS IT WITH HONEY
A HUNDRED YEARS LATER AN ARABIAN MARE
GRAZING ON THE STEPPES OF HIS LONGING
BREAKS HER OWN RECORD SPEED
A DEAFMUTE READS HIS REFUSAL AND FEELS LOVED
A ONE-EYED MILKMAN JOGGING HIS HORSES OVER THE SNOW
WARMS HIS HANDS AT THE PENITENT TONGUES OF THE STARS

THE POET WRITES MANY LETTERS

Bills for horses he never bought,
an inventory of stars,
a plea for his left leg;
he answers them all
so beautifully that the stableman
saves the letter and hangs it over his bed,
the air saves the invoice and says it aloud,
the one-legged beggar saves his rejection
and eats it with honey.
A hundred years later an Arabian mare
grazing on the steppes of his longing
breaks her own record speed.
A deaf-mute reads his refusal and feels loved.
A one-eyed milkman jogging his horses over the snow
warms his hands at the penitent tongues of stars.

THE POET ELECTS HIMSELF PRESIDENT

Looking about him,
seeing no one more qualified
he elected himself head of the land.
On his arms, ships glided to the sea.
On his navel, the capital raised its dome.
His back supported a lawn, croquet, and decisions.
There were slums and mothers-in-law.
And far overhead he heard the rioting of the stars.
He summoned a net from his hair.
"I will rid the sky of these strangers."
Then the foot said to the head,
Step down, brother, you are no better
than I. The poet impeached himself,
ate black bread, smoked a little, and spoke
in proverbs to delight the young.

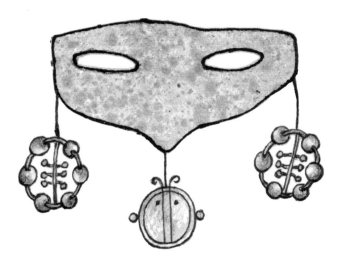

THE POET ENTERS THE SLEEP OF THE BEES

Turning to honey one morning, I passed
through their glass cells and entered
the sleep of the bees.
The bees were making a lexicon
of the six-sided names of God,

clover's breath, dewflesh,
ritual of the thorn, a definitive work
to graft the names to their roots.
For days I hiked over their sleepshod sounds.
At last I saw a green lion
eating a hole in the sun,

and a red dragon burning itself alive
to melt the snow that lay like a cap
on the sleep of the bees.
Their sleep was a factory
of sweetness with no author.

Every syllable was swept clean,
every act was without motive.
Please forgive me this poor translation.
How could I hold
my past to my present when I heard
ten thousand tongues flowing along like gold?

THE POET FOLDS TO HIS HEART
A THOUSAND WOMEN

To the convent he comes, his poems fluttering
on ribbons and shoelaces.
He tells them how buffalos dance,
he tells them he is a buffalo
and he dances on the knuckles of his toes.
He tells them there are apes in hell,
he tells them he is an ape
waiting on table at the Lord's Supper.
He pushes two fingers in his mouth
and whistles,
he rides the sun into the hunt,
he is the hunter and the whipper-in,
yes, and the dogs, the fiddler and fiddle,
the ape and garden,
their snow and water;
the man and woman,
with heavy hair and a soft chest.
He wears tall boots, he has a hole in his tooth
big enough to hide a daughter.

THE POET TURNS HIS ENEMY
INTO A PAIR OF WINGS

His enemy was a dragon laced with medals.
It picked his pockets, hid his poems,
beat its tail on his head at night,
blew the nose off his wife's face.
For God's sake, peace! cried the poet.
Then the dragon jumped on his back.
Warm in his lizardskin coat he stepped outside.
No one, no one else in the snowy city
wore a lizardskin coat!
Its purple hearts jingled like temple bells.
It rested its pointed chin on the poet's head.
Go right, said the dragon.
The poet skipped left.
Go up, said the dragon.
The poet went downtown.
At one o'clock it turned yellow.
At two o'clock it turned green.
Go up, said the dragon, or let me be.
I am Salamander, fireman of the stars,
bound to cross my brow with their ashes.
How shall I go? asked the poet.
Just as you are, said the dragon,
day in night, night in hand,
hand in pocket, pocket in poem,
poem in bone, bone in flesh!
flesh in flight.

THE POET LOSES HIS NAME IN A WELL

The poet bent over to drink
and his name slipped into the well.
A man at the bottom caught it,
and called to the sun,

"I am a poor peddler. Bending to drink
I fell, pulled by the weight
of all that I couldn't let go.
Oh, my forks and rubies, my scissors and books,

my bells and apples and red mouths!
They hang on me like a brace of anchors.
Poet, teach me to walk
naked as a new planet."

The poet whistled. He called himself
to come out of the twilight.
His name swam up like a dog.
Clean as a pebble, the peddler
sang in its jaws.

PUTTING HIS FINGER IN THE DYKE,
HE SAVES ALL HOLLAND

Passing the dyke, he hears someone call him:

a voice from a mouth in the dyke,
a hole which he plugs with his arm.

His sister brings him his meals.
His right hand lifts the spoon

and his left hand ruffles
the last cries of the drowned.

His mother reads him his letters
asking for fingerprints and a blessing

while his right hand signs checks
and his left hand smoothes the hair

of a dead baby. The mayor gives him
a medal for keeping the peace:

> *This is the poet who saved a city,*
> *who offered himself to our enemy the sea,*
>
> *the sea who feeds us and maims us,*
> *who covers over the words of our fathers*
>
> *and torments us with shipwrecks and bad dreams.*
> *This is the poet who took on himself*
>
> *our bad dreams and made them beautiful,*
> *our fathers' secrets and made them ours.*

THE POET TRACKS DOWN THE MOON

In the woods, the old moon is barking
and humming and turning around on her nest.
The poet calls his dogs and carries
a net to catch her, this quartz quail,
this silver truffle slivering into the dark.

When the moon hears him, she turns out her light,
leaves her skin under a bush like patience,
and covers her tracks with a sigh.
To the river she throws the first letter
of her language, the crescent, the open trap.

It stands for *canny* and *clever*. She throws it
like bread to catch the poet who at once
swims into her net. When he walks, the moon
hangs her thin wire around his ankle,
hangs her tiny hook in the gills of his heart.

THE BAKER'S WIFE TELLS HIS HOROSCOPE WITH PRETZELS

At dawn he visits the baker's wife
in her Tenth Street kitchen.
Already the ovens are hot.
Already a bride and groom stand up
on the plain face of heaven.
Already birthdays write themselves
on the chocolate cheeks of the moon.

The baker's wife, powdered with fine stars,
ties back the future with pretzels,
hundreds of pretzels crossing their arms in prayer.

"In the house of the archer I see you
teaching the sun to heel.
Though the moon cancels the sign of the two fish,
though she locks the sun in the house of the crab,
though she draws off the nations in tides of folly,
for you the lamb will lie down with the lion,
the virgin will put her head in your lap."

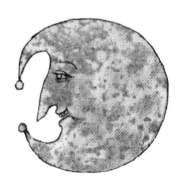

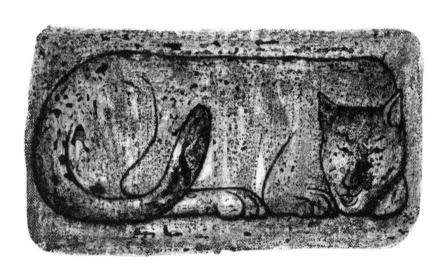

TWO HUNDRED CATS APPLY THEIR TONGUES FOR HIS BATH

All winter he dreams of a wise book
written on tablets
borne on the tails of white mice.

There he reads of the tongues
of cats, harsher than files,

"as that with licking
they will wear out the skin
of a man." Now he stands

at his window and calls
for two hundred Hassidic cats.

From all parts of the city
they dance to him, on broomsticks
and feathers and false teeth,

to lick their lore into his blood.
Every winter the poet grows heavy with sleep.

Every spring his own body astounds him.
His old skin unravels,
he knits it into a new song.

THE POET STUMBLES UPON
THE ASTRONOMER'S ORCHARDS

Once a scholar showed me the sky.
He held up a grapefruit:
here is the sun.
He held up an orange:
this is the harvest moon.
If you watch my hands, you will see
how the sun stays in its socket,
how the earth turns, how the moon
ripens and falls and swells again.

Under an axle tree, I took my seat.
The leaves were stars
juggling pineapples and pears.
                              What a show!
A thousand lemons are rolling through space,
avocados nudge down the rings of Jupiter
and coconuts shake the galaxy to its teeth
till the tree loses its leaves.

But there is a star in my apple when I cut it
and some hungry traveler is paring the moon away.

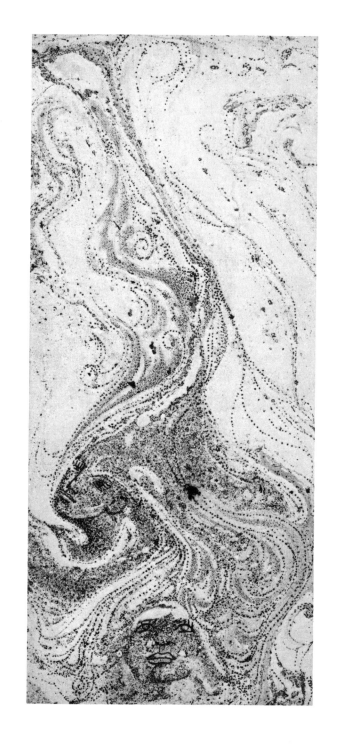

THE POET'S WIFE WATCHES HIM
ENTER THE EYE OF THE SNOW

She knew he was writing a poem
because everything in the room
was slowly sifting away:
her dustpan the color of buttercups,
her eyeglasses and her sink
and her five masks praising the sun.

That night she saw him ascend.
He floated above their bed,
he gathered the dark strands
of the poem like a tide.

On his nose her glasses polished
themselves to crystals. On his back
the dustpan fanned out
like a saffron cape.
Now he was turning his face toward the sun
and riding her simple sink into heaven.

In the morning she calls to the newsboy:
"How can I, wife of the poet
know what he saw and did there?
It is enough that I open my eyes

and my glasses perch on my nose
and show me the brittle dreams of parrots.
Enough that my dustpan believes it shoulders
the broken bones of those warriors the stars,
that my sink gurgles for joy,
and my five masks tell me more
than I knew when I made them."

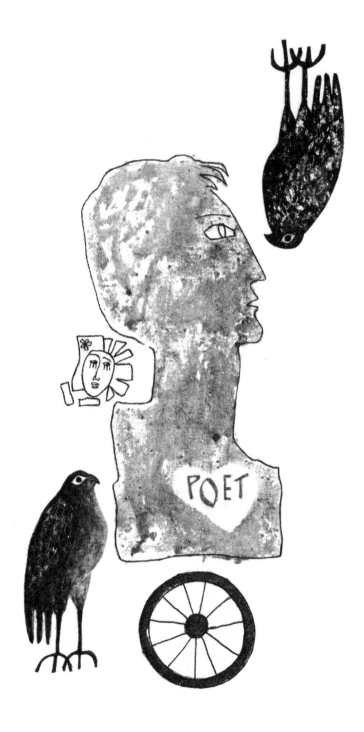

THE POET'S WIFE MAKES HIM A DOOR SO HE CAN FIND THE WAY HOME.

Nobody else makes doors like the poet's wife.

If she made a revolving door,
summer and winter would run like mice in a wheel.
If she made a door for the moon,
the dead would cross over alive.

Each door is a mirror.

So when the poet loses his way,
crossing the desert in search of his heart,
his wife hoists her lintels and straw on her back
and sets out, feeling his grief with her feet.

She calls up a door that shimmers like water.

She unfolds her palm trees and parrots.
And far away, his belly dredging the dunes,
the poet hears his heart spinning
straw into gold for the sun.

The palms bow. The parrots are calling his name.

He remembers the way home.

The original drawings were done in ink with pen and brush
on watercolor paper and linen paper.
The text type is Janson, set by Thompson Type, San Diego, California.
The display type is Weiss Roman, set by Thompson Type,
and Palatino Italic with Swash,
set by Franklin Photolettering Inc., New York, New York.
Printed by Rae Publishing Co., Inc., Cedar Grove, New Jersey.
Bound by The Book Press, Brattleboro, Vermont.